ANCIENT HEBREW ARTS

ANCIENT HEBREW ARTS

A. REIFENBERG

SCHOCKEN BOOKS / NEW YORK

ANCIENT HEBREW ARTS

Pp. 51 to 57, halftitle and running heads: *for* The Hellenistic Period *read* The Persian and Hellenistic Periods

P. 147, No. 4 and P. 167: *add* Collection Miriam Schaar Schloessinger (Mrs. Max Schloessinger) Jerusalem

INTRODUCTION

ARCHAEOLOGY is centuries old. It began during the periods of the Renaissance and Humanism when scholars and collectors became intensely interested in the material survivals of Greek and Roman antiquity. A first requisite for the expansion of archaeology to new fields was provided when in 1799 the Rosetta stone was discovered and its trilingual inscription furnished the key to the understanding of the Egyptian language. Three years later, three names in Cuneiform were read for the first time. About thirty years later the systematic decipherment of Assyrian inscriptions began.

A milestone in biblical archaeology was the recovery in 1870 of the Mesha stone. Written in a language almost identical with Hebrew, the inscription confirmed and elaborated on the biblical report, II Kings 1 and 3, which tells of the conquest of Moab by Omri and Ahab, the Kings of Israel in the 9th century. From a slow start biblical archaeology grew into a science with refined methods and unexpectedly rich results. As excavations bore fruit it became evident that many of their finds lent support to the authenticity of important parts of the Bible.

This volume presents remains of Jewish antiquity. It offers, from what was preserved or has been restored to us by excavations, a selection which conveys an ample impression of the art and useful objects created in Palestine during the biblical period and in the early Jewish Diaspora.

The remains cover a span of about 2,000 years, from the time of the

Kings to the 6th or 7th century C.E. The early examples belong to a period when Israelites were entirely dependent on neighboring peoples. Foreign civilizations, Hittite, Egyptian, Phoenician, Mesopotamian, and Aegean, sent their products into Palestine. In the time of the Kings, art and applied art made remarkable progress toward the development of an authentically Hebraic expression and productivity. Though many of the objects of this period were patterned after pagan precedents, there already appears the distinct character of a Hebrew culture.

In 722, Samaria, the capital of Israel, fell into the hands of the Assyrians. In 586 Jerusalem was destroyed by the Babylonians. In the period following, the influence of the Greek mainland is felt for the first time in Jewish civilization. The Greek element became increasingly stronger in the subsequent centuries. But while there prevailed the threat of a complete predominance of Hellenistic culture and Greco-Roman forms and themes, a genuine Jewish art expression took shape, with indigenous motives, and these lasted through Herodian times.

To be sure, the material remains of Jewish antiquity from the period of the Maccabees are modest, but they have significance as the foundation of synagogue art. The products of the first centuries C.E. were closely connected with Jewish ideology and Jewish ritual. They represent a marked contribution to the development of Jewish art, made their impression on the Jewish Middle Ages and are part of Jewish art consciousness to this day. Influences exerted by Jewish antiquities beyond the national confines or upon later developments had their beginnings before the period of synagogue art. Hebrew motives pervaded not only the Greek world but later Jewish antiquity and early Christian art. The lions guarding the law and the winged angels of Christianity derive alike from the biblical cherubim; the Hebrew-Phoenician script is the parent of the Greek and Latin alphabets. The seven-branched candlestick, the Menorah, which first appeared in the time of the Maccabees, became a symbol of Judaism throughout the Diaspora. The lulav (a plant combination) and ethrog (a citrus fruit), the emblems of Sukkot (Feast of Tabernacles), which are met with in representations of the same period, became themes favored through the ages.

10

The influence of Jewish synagogue art reaches deeper. It forms the connecting link between antiquity and Christian-Byzantine architecture. In the synagogue secular pagan architecture was first adapted to the religious needs of a non-pagan community. The architectural details and particular architectonic features of the Christian basilicas occurred previously in the synagogue. Jewish pictorial synagogue art influenced the art of the Christian church.

It is probable that future finds and research will result in many corrections of currently held opinions. However, it appears certain that they will maintain or strengthen the thesis that an authentic expression, genuinely Hebraic ideas and motives, is found in the remains of Jewish antiquity and that here as elsewhere early Judaism exerted its influence upon other cultures and peoples.

THE PERIOD OF THE KINGS

ISRAELITE HISTORY in Palestine begins about 1220 B.C.E. when the Israelite tribes invaded the country and began the conquest of the native populace. At this time, however, Palestine's history already embraced more than 3,000 preceding years and its prehistory reached back over a series of cultures which had endured for thousands of years.

The evidences for the pre-Israelite history of Palestine, partly reflected in the biblical tales, were uncovered in the progress of the same archaeological work which had resulted in the remarkable finds from Hebrew culture. Once the archaeologists had developed methods to determine the chronology of the different strata, excavations in Palestine laid open a vast range, from the earliest appearances of man and man's activities to civilizations for which archaeological as well as other kind of historical evidence is ample.

A Stone Age civilization, developed by a grain-cultivating people, had existed in Palestine about 6000 B.C.E. It was called the Natufian. And while other cultures had preceded, it was the first to yield sufficient finds for the drawing of a somewhat precise picture. The Natufian is followed by the Neolithic age (5000-4000) when Palestinian man began to build permanent settlements. The important towns of the country, Jericho, Jerusalem, Gezer, Megiddo, originated in that period.

At the end of the Stone Age (3000) Palestine, due to her strategic position, became a meeting place of migrants and invaders from Babylonia and Egypt. In the following centuries, highly developed Semitic and Egyptian cultures met and blended in the cities and on the commercial and military roads of Palestine. Egyptian, Phoenician, Cretan, Cypriot, Syrian and other Asia Minor influences shaped the urban civilization of Palestine. Architecture and crafts were on a high level.

When the Israelites entered Palestine, they did not as yet possess the desire and capacities for a more complex cultural life. A change came about early in the period of the Kings, with which begins our presentation of Hebrew and Jewish ancient arts.

EZION-GEBER

on the Red Sea near Elath, the present Aqabah, was the seaport of King Solomon (973-933 B.C.E.). "King Solomon made a navy of ships in Ezion-geber, which is beside Elath in the land of Edom. . . . Once every three years came the navy of Tarshish, bringing gold, and silver, ivory, and apes and peacocks . . . plenty of sandal-wood and precious stones" (I Kings 9:26; 10:22,11).

The furnaces and refineries of Ezion-geber which smelted the copper ore found in the neighborhood added to the wealth of Solomon and helped bring prosperity to the country in his time.

Houses of stone and brick buildings, for dwelling and industrial purposes, were uncovered at Ezion-geber.

Excavated by the American School of Oriental Research.

THE STABLES OF KING SOLOMON

uncovered with other public buildings at Megiddo, accommodated about 500 horses. The hitching posts (I Kings 9:15-19) carried the mangers and supported the roof. Also found was a 120-yard-long tunnel which had been driven through the rock to connect a spring outside the fortress with a 180-foot-deep shaft inside from where the city received its water. Excavated by the Oriental Institute of the University of Chicago.

RECONSTRUCTION OF THE STABLES

by Professor E. L. Sukenik, Hebrew University, Jerusalem.

VOLUTE CAPITALS

These "Phoenician" volute capitals, about 1 m long, forerunners of Ionic capitals, were found at Megiddo. King Solomon was advised by Tyrian architects; thus these capitals in all probability are similar to architectural details of the Temple.

Excavated by the Oriental Institute of the University of Chicago; now at the Archaeological Museum, Jerusalem.

TOMB MONUMENT AT JERUSALEM

hewn out of rock, upon the eastern side of the Kidron valley opposite the
Temple Square, probably the only detached building which survived from
the period of the Kings; 12 feet high, 18 feet long.

Originally the door must have been lower, since in raising it there has been
destroyed an inscription of which today there remain but two letters. The
lettering shows that the tomb dates from the time of the Kings. The hollow
groove design (cavetto), the cornice, and the walls sloping slightly inwards
resemble the Egyptian mortuary chapels and altars of the Amarna age
(c.1400 B.C.E.) and later periods.

TOWN GATE OF MIZPAH (TEL EN NASBEH)

The gate (about 4 m) of this Israelite city shows an open court with stone benches along the walls. Benches are also affixed to the town gate itself. Sitting "in the gate" the judges administered justice (Deut. 21:19, Amos 5, 15: etc.); the gate was the public meeting place, there the market was held (II Kings 7:1) and strangers were welcomed.

Mizpah played an important role in Israelite history. At Mizpah the Israelites assembled under the leadership of Samuel (Judg. 20:1; I Sam. 10:17); after the destruction of Jerusalem, Mizpah was the residence of the governor of Judea (II Kings 25:23; Jer. 40:6;41:16).

Excavated by the Pacific School of Religion, Berkeley, California.

FROM THE PALACES OF OMRI AND
AHAB AT SAMARIA

The palaces of King Omri (887-876) and King Ahab (876-853) had imposing and well-built walls. The details of the work showing in the remains of the outer walls of the palaces indicate the progress of architecture in the period of the Kings. The stones are faced and laid regularly as headers and stretchers. Stones of this kind, with bosses, were also found at Megiddo and Beth-shan.
Excavated by Harvard University.

THE SILOAM (OR SHILOAH) TUNNEL

is a masterpiece of ancient engineering. It conducted the waters from the spring of Gihon, outside of Jerusalem's walls, to the inner city. The tunnel was constructed under King Hezekiah in about 700 B.C.E. (II Kings 20:20). It is over 500 yards long and was designed to supply water for the city in the event of a siege.

THE SILOAM INSCRIPTION

A Hebrew inscription was found in the Siloam (or Shiloah) Tunnel (see
p. 22) and it tells how the miners, having begun work at both ends, were
guided by the sound of the stone picks and finally met in the center: "(This
is the) tunnel. And this was the story of the tunnel: While yet (the miners
were lifting up) the pick, each toward his fellow, and while yet there were
three cubits [about 1½ yds.] to be bored through (there was hear)d the
voice of each (c)alling to his fellow, for there was a split in the rock on the
right hand and on (the left ha)nd. And on the day of the boring through, the
miners struck, each to meet his fellow, pick upon (p)ick; and there flowed
the waters from the source to the pool for two hundred and a thousand cubits;
and a hundred cubits was the height of the rock above the head of the
miner(s)."[1]

Istanbul Museum.

1]

. . . הנקבה. וזה. היה. דבר. הנקבה. בעוד . . .
הגרזן. אש. אל. רעו. ובעוד. שלש. אמת. להנקוב. נשמ[ע]. קל. אש. ק
רא. אל. רעו. כי. הית. זדה. בצר. מימן . . . . א. ובים. ה
נקבה. הכו. החצבם. אש. לקרת. רעו. גרזן. עלו. גרזן. וילכו
המים. מן. המוצא. אל. הברכה. במאתים. ואלף. אמה. ומא
ת. אמה. היה. גבה. הצר. על. ראש. החצבם

BRONZE STAND FROM MEGIDDO

depicting in openwork-cut style (à jour technique) the invocation of a god seated upon a throne (c. 1000 B.C.E.). The basins in the Temple of Solomon rested on bronze stands and it may well be that they resembled this stand dug from the Megiddo mound.

Evidences of religious worship at Megiddo are numerous; this bronze stand is one among many others. *Half the actual size.*

Excavated by the Oriental Institute of the University of Chicago; now at the Archaeological Museum, Jerusalem.

IVORIES FROM SAMARIA

THE IVORY PLAQUES on pp. 25-29 are remains of the "ivory house" built by King Ahab (876-853) in Samaria (I Kings 22:39). They are inlaid with gold, lapis lazuli, and stones of many colors, and glass. They served as coverings for walls, furniture and other household goods.

All of them show the influence of Phoenician art, into which had entered Egyptian, northern Syrio-Hittite and Assyrian elements. Phoenician craftsmen introduced this style to Israel.

Closely related to these ivory tablets are the earlier ivory carvings from Megiddo and those from Nimrud and Arslan Tash which are almost contemporaneous.

Excavated by a joint expedition of Harvard University, the Hebrew University in Jerusalem, the Palestine Exploration Fund, the British Academy, and the British School of Archaeology in Jerusalem; now at the Archaeological Museum, Jerusalem.

A woman's head (Astarte) at a window.
Approximately actual size.

IVORY PLAQUE FROM SAMARIA

This carving shows a cherub astride the stem of a plant. Solomon's Temple contained "graved cherubim, lions and palm-trees . . . with wreaths round about" (I Kings 7:36). Two mighty cherubim, about sixteen feet in height, carved from olive wood and gilded, stood in the Holy of Holies. In Phoenician art King Ahiram of Byblos was portrayed on a throne supported by cherubim. The God of Israel was thought of as "sitting upon the cherubim" (I Sam. 4:4, etc.). However, in accordance with the requirements of the Israelite religion, representations of God were never shown. *One and one-half the actual size.*
Archaeological Museum, Jerusalem.

IVORY PLAQUE FROM SAMARIA

The Egyptian god Horus crouching upon a lotus. In Samaria, predominantly Egyptian themes were found, such as Horus, and kneeling figures of
other gods. *Approximately actual size.*
Archaeological Museum, Jerusalem.

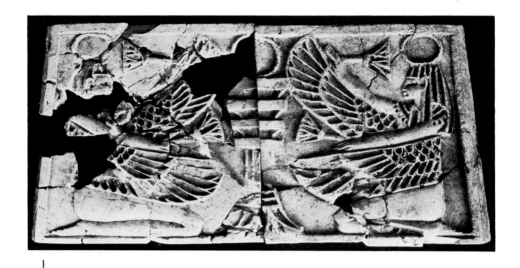

1

IVORY PLAQUES FROM SAMARIA

1   Winged goddesses, probably Isis and Nephtys, flanking an Osiris symbol. *Approximately one and one-half the actual size.*

2   Fight between a lion and a bull. *Approximately one and one-half the actual size.*

3   The Egyptian god Rah in a squatting position, with palm leaves and the sign of life; along the upper rim a chain of Phoenician palmettos broken by a solar disk above the head of the god. *Actual size.*

4   Palm tree motif; the walls and doors of the Temple of Solomon were decorated with such motifs (II Chron. 3:5). *Actual size.*

Archaeological Museum, Jerusalem.

2

3

4

SEALS

THE SEALS of the period of the Kings (8th to 6th centuries B.C.E.) show high artistic perfection and the same style that appears in the ivory carvings. This glyptic art was not confined to Israel, but is found also among the other Canaanite peoples, the Phoenicians, Ammonites, Moabites and Edomites.

Seals for letters and documents were widely used in pre-Israelite times. Generally, however, they were not name-seals but merely representations of mythological scenes, geometrical ornaments, etc. The personal name-seal was first used in Canaan; the addition of names was more customary in Israel than among neighboring peoples. Mere name-seals, that is, without any pictorial representation, were almost exclusively found in Judea, where the pagan influence was much weaker than in Israel. Possibly the increasing use of the inscribed seal indicates a growing awareness of religious prohibitions.

Most of the names are combinations containing the name of God, *El* or *Yahu*, later abbreviated to *Yah*. On the inscribed seals appear preponderantly names known to us from the books of Ezra and Nehemiah. Hence, we can ascribe a number of the seals to the Persian period.

The seals, mostly scarabs in imitation of the oval Egyptian beetle, or of scarab form, were generally worn upon a cord around the neck (Gen. 38:18), on the arm (Cant. 8:6), or on the hand (Jer. 22:24). The materials were usually semiprecious stones, such as cornelian, onyx, rock crystal, jasper, amethyst, lapis lazuli; ivory and other materials were also used. The engraving was done with a diamond-set stylus (Jer. 17:1).

The pictorial themes show the influence of the mixed Phoenician culture. Also, there are found such Egyptian motifs as griffins, the child Horus, symbols of life and the snake of uraeus, the cherub, animals, sacrificial scenes, the winged solar disk, palmettos, etc.

SEALS

1   Winged being with Egyptian crown and scorpion's tail, at left the Horus falcon with solar disk (symbol of the sun god) on a stand, inscribed "Belonging to Ahimelech."[1] *Twice the actual size.*

2   Cherub (winged lion with man's head) wearing an apron across the forelegs, inscribed "Pedael"[2] (probably Phoenician). *Four times the actual size.*

3   Winged griffin with Egyptian double crown and symbol of life, in lower part a locust, inscribed "Belonging to Haman"[3] (from Megiddo). *Twice the actual size.*

4   Crouching winged griffin, as in 3, inscribed "Belonging to Hayyim"[4] (from Tell Far'a, the ancient Beth-pelet, near Gaza). *Twice the actual size.*

5   Recumbent griffin, as in 3, above winged solar disk, inscribed "Belonging to Rafa"[5] (probably Phoenician). *Twice the actual size.*

1, 3 and 4 at the Archaeological Museum, Jerusalem; 2 and 5 from the author's collection.

1] לאחימלך   2] פדאל   3] לחמן   4] לחים   5] לרפא

1

2

4

3

SEALS

1 Walking man, long-haired and bearded, holding a staff in his hand; above the staff a crescent and solar disk; inscribed "Belonging to Pera."[1] (Probably Phoenician.)

2 Sacrificial scene; the hand of the sacrificer is raised in the gesture of adoration, the animal possibly represents an ibex; inscribed "Belonging to Elsmachi"[2] ("God is my support").

3 The Egyptian symbol of life in the upper, a winged serpent in the lower section; inscribed "Belonging to Abiyu"[3] ("God is my father"). (From Galilee.)

4 Winged scarab; inscribed "Belonging to Elnatan."[4] (From Syria.)

All reproductions twice the actual size.

From the author's collection.

———

1] לפרע 2] לאלסמחי 3] לאביו 4] לאלנתן

2

1

SEALS

1 Winged scarab and the Egyptian symbol of life; inscribed "Belonging to Ahimelech"[1] in the lower segment, "Samach"[2] in the upper, probably meaning in its entirety "Belonging to Ahimelech [son of] Samach." (From Lachish.) *Twice the actual size.*

Found during the excavations of the Wellcome Archaeological Research Expedition at Tel Duweir (Lachish); now at the Palestine Archaeological Museum, Jerusalem.

2 Walking man, holding a staff, behind him a serpent whose tail coils around a stand and on the stand a rooster; the head of the man shows Egyptian, his costume Mesopotamian influence; inscribed "Shemab,"[3] a name probably meaning "The father hears." *Twice the actual size.*

From the author's collection.

3 Seal in original copper casing: ram; inscribed "Belonging to Jotham."[4] (From Ezion-geber.) *One and one-half the actual size.*

Found during the excavations of the American School of Oriental Research at Ezion-geber; now at the Smithsonian Institution, Washington, D.C.

1] לאחימלך   2] סמך   3] שמאב   4] ליתם

3

1

2

SEALS

1 Egyptian symbols, inscribed "Belonging to Ashna, the servant of Ahaz."[1] Ashna was an official of King Ahaz of Judah (736-721). *Greatly enlarged.*

Edward T. Newell Collection.

2 Roaring lion, inscribed "Belonging to Shema, servant of Jeroboam,"[2] .037 m long, .027 m wide, .017 m thick (jasper, from Megiddo); Shema was a minister of King Jeroboam II (785-745).

Formerly at the Istanbul Museum; now lost.

1] לאשנא עבד אחז   2] לשמע עבד ירבעם

GOLD RING WITH HEBREW SEAL

Winged uraeus (serpent) with crown of Upper Egypt, beneath it a papyrus on stalk; inscribed "Belonging to Shaphat"[1] (from Palestine). *Twice the actual size.*

From the Richmond Collection, Haifa.

1] לשפט

SEAL

RING

1

2

SEALS

1   Fighting cock, inscribed "Belonging to Jaazaniahu, the servant of the King,"[1] probably referring to Jaazaniah, the son of the Maacathite, one of the "captains of the forces" (II Kings 25:23) and commander of Mizpah (onyx, from Tel en Nasbeh, i.e. Mizpah). *Twice the actual size.*
Excavated by the Pacific School of Religion, Berkeley, Cal.

2   Name-seal, inscribed "Belonging to Hoshayahu, the son of Shelem-yahu"[2] (from the vicinity of Jerusalem). This seal without any pictorial representation and with its elegantly executed inscription is characteristic of Judean seals. *Four times the actual size.*
From the author's collection.

———

לאזניהו עבד המלך [1   2] להושעיהו בן שלמיהו [1

NAME SEALS

1   Inscribed "Belonging to Rabbiyahu, [the son of] Higlaniyah";[1] if the
name, meaning "God exiled me," refers to the Babylonian exile, it can be
assumed that Rabbiyahu was born in the third quarter of the 6th century.
2   Inscribed "Belonging to Aliyah, the slave-wife of Hananel"[2] (from
Amman); women used seals in their own right.

HEBREW WEIGHT STONE

Inscribed *Beka*,[3] that is "One-half" [shekel]. In ancient Israel silver was
not minted but weighed; merchants carried a scale and a bag filled with
weight stones (Prov. 16:11; Deut. 25:13). The designation *beka* is known
from the Bible (Gen. 24:22; Exod. 38:26). *All pictures twice the actual size.*
From the author's collection.

בקע [3   לעליה אמת חננאל [2   לרביהו הגלניה [1

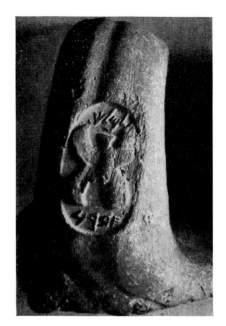

1   2

JAR-HANDLE STAMPS

Earthenware jars, gauged as measures and probably serving for the collection of taxes in kind, carried the "royal property" stamp and the name of the city, either the capital of an administrative district or the seat of a royal potter's workshop. Several hundreds of such jar-handle stamps, dating from the last centuries of the Judean monarchy, have been found.

1   Winged solar disk, inscribed "Belonging to the King, [city of] Sochoh."[1] *Actual size.*

From the author's collection.

2   Winged scarab, inscribed "Belonging to the King, [city of] Hebron."[2] *Actual size.*

Archaeological Museum, Jerusalem.

---

[1] למלך שוכה   [2] למלך חברון

CERAMICS

THE EARLIEST Israelite ceramics scarcely differ from Canaanite wares; the indigenous Canaanite civilization continued to exercise its influence. Many pieces of pottery appear to be copies of imports. Imports from Cyprus are found, as are imitations of Cypriot forms. The Philistine influence often appears in the painting of vessels with rings. Faience was imported from Egypt. But besides imports and imitations there exists the work of Israelite potters which reveals genuine artistry and high skill.

1   Pot for cooking (from Beth-shemesh) .115 m high.
2   Small jug, possibly an import from Cyprus, .09 m high.
3,4   Jugs, apparently copies of imported metal jugs (from Beth-shemesh) .13 and .11 m high.
From the author's collection.

1   2

CERAMICS

1   Libation bowl (from a tomb near Hebron) .17 m high.

2   Jug, typically Israelite, and an example of fine Israelite craftsmanship, .2 m high.

From the author's collection.

3   Lamp, diameter: .125 m; like all lamps of the Israelite period it has a more firmly curved mouth than lamps of the pre-Israelite period; the Israelite lamps often possess a base.

From the author's collection.

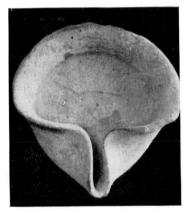

3

ASTARTE FIGURINES

ASTARTE, the Queen of Heaven, was the goddess most frequently represented among the Canaanites. Many of the Israelites who had entered Canaan adopted the cult of the goddess, together with the forms of her appearance. The Bible reports even of Solomon that he followed Astarte, the goddess of the Sidonians. To the people of Palestine Astarte was the goddess of procreation and fertility. Her images, representations for example of Astarte as a nursing mother, were probably used as amulets.

The primitive representations of Astarte are very roughly done. The body forms and contours are merely indicated, no more than to make them recognizable as the characteristics of a female deity. But subsequently the representations are influenced by Babylonian, Cypriot, Phoenician, and Egyptian prototypes. The execution becomes more distinct and specific; individual situations and positions are clearly portrayed. The influence of three different cultures can often be noted in one and the same object.

Hebrew religion prohibits pictorial or sculptural representation, and indeed no such representation of the biblical God has been found. Animals, modeled in clay, are however frequent. In Jericho, Israelite already in the earliest times, scarcely any idols of any kind have been discovered; but the excavations at Beth-shemesh and in other places show clearly that despite all religious prohibitions (Deut. 27:15) animal and human figures were modeled by the Israelites. The Astarte figurines found in different places add further evidence of the circumvention of the biblical prohibition under the influence of Canaanite religion.

ASTARTE FIGURINES

1,2   with lotus flowers; the exaggerated hips show Phoenician, the lotus flowers Egyptian influence in theme and style; figurine no. 2 dates from Iron Age I, c. 1200-1000 B.C.E.

3   Astarte with a tiara, similar to Babylonian types (from Megiddo) .114 m high.

From the author's collection.

ASTARTE FIGURINE 1

pillar-shaped, .175 m high, Iron Age II (c. 800 B.C.E.) (from a tomb near Hebron); the emphasis on the breasts denotes Astarte as a symbol of fertility.

From the author's collection.

JUG 2

shaped like a human figure, .135 m high (from Gezer); the features of the face are distinctly Semitic.

Excavated by the Palestine Exploration Fund; now at the Palestine Archaeological Museum, Jerusalem.

1   2

RIDER

Probably one of the oldest representations of a horseman (Iron Age II, c. 800 B.C.E.), .12 m high (from a grave near Hebron); the treatment is reminiscent of Hittite prototypes; remains of the original coloring are still recognizable.

From the author's collection.

STONE ALTAR

for incense, with horns at four corners (from Megiddo, c. 1000 B.C.E.); such altars are frequently found in Palestine. The "horns of the altar" were a place of refuge (I Kings 1:50;2:28). *Approximately one-fifth of actual size.*

Excavated by the Oriental Institute of the University of Chicago; now at the Archaeological Museum, Jerusalem.

OSTRACA

THE ART of writing was widespread in ancient Israel. This is evidenced by the large number of inscribed potsherds (ostraca) from the 8th to the 6th centuries which have been discovered. Potsherds usually served the purpose of our note paper. Writing was also done on papyrus, but outside Egypt writing on papyrus disintegrated under the influence of the climate.

1   Ostracon (from Samaria, 8th century), inscribed in Hebrew:
                "Baruch, greetings
                Baruch, this time pay attention and
                (give....., the son of)
                Yimnah, barley, 13 (measures)"[1]
The writing is scratched into the sherd. *Actual size.*
Excavated by a joint expedition of Harvard University, the Hebrew University in Jerusalem, the Palestine Exploration Fund, the British Academy, and the British School of Archaeology in Jerusalem; now at the Archaeological Museum, Jerusalem.
2   Bowl (from Beth-shemesh), carrying the burnt-in inscription "Thy brother."[2] *Actual size.*
Excavated by the Palestine Exploration Fund; now at the Archaeological Museum, Jerusalem.

אחך [2   ברוך שלם ברך הפעם הקשב ו . . . . . ימנה שערם [XIII] [1

1

2

A LACHISH LETTER

Report from Hoshayahu, a subaltern, to Yaush, the commandant of the fortress of Lachish, 589 B.C.E.

This is one of the nineteen letters, written in classical Hebrew, the "first personal documents in pre-exilic Hebrew writing found in Palestine," remarkable because of their "clear writing, beautiful language and highly important contents." They were discovered in the guardroom of the gate of the border fortress of Lachish, a town in the hills of Judea, about twelve miles west of Hebron, which dominated the road from Gaza to Hebron. The letters, written with pen and ink, date from the time of the prophet Jeremiah, when "the king of Babylon's army fought . . . against Lachish and against Azekah; for these alone remained of the cities of Judah as fortified cities" (Jer. 34:7).

The Lachish letters, most of which are reports to the commandant of the fortress from Hoshayahu, who was in command of one of the posts close to the town, are from the late summer of 589 B.C.E., shortly before the arrival of the main Babylonian army that invested Jerusalem a year later.

The letter here reproduced reads: "May YHWH cause my lord to hear this very day tidings of good! And now, according to everything that my lord has written, this has thy servant done. I have written on the door according to all that my lord has sent me. And with regard to what my lord has sent about the matter of the guest house — there is nobody there. And as for Semachiah, Shemaiah has taken him and has brought him up to the city [Jerusalem]. And as for thy servant I am not sending thither anyone [?] today [?] but in the course of the [coming] morning (I will send?). And (my lord) will know that we are watching for the signals of Lachish according to all the indications which my lord has given, for we cannot see (the signals) of Azekah."[1] (Translation according to H. N. Torczyner, as amended by C. H. Gordon, H. G. May, and W. F. Albright.)

Excavated by the Wellcome Archaeological Research Expedition; now at the Archaeological Museum, Jerusalem.

---

[1] Obverse: ישמע. יהוה.]את[אדני עת כים שמעת טב. ועת ככל אשר שלח אדני
כן. עשה עבדך כתבתי על הדלת ככל אשר שלח אדני אלי. וכי. שלח אדני. על
דבר בית הרפד אין שם אדם וסמכיהו לקחה. שמעיהו ויעלהו העירה ועבדך
אדני ישלח שמה איהו

Reverse: כי אם. בתסבתה בקר וידע כי אל. משאת לכש. נחנו שמרם בכל האתת
אשר נתן אדני. כי לא נראה את עזקה

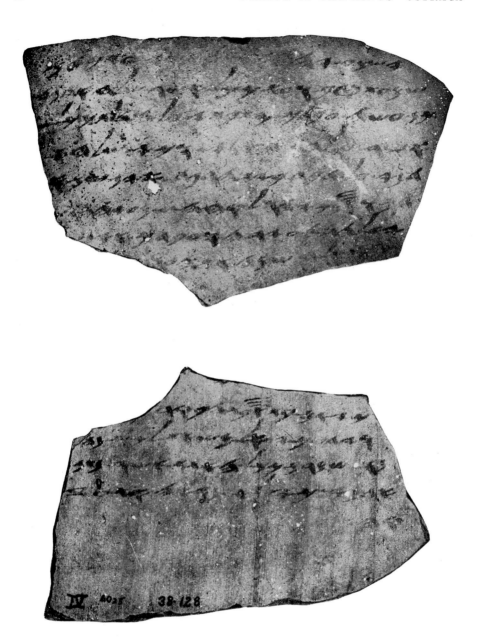

THE HELLENISTIC PERIOD

REMAINS OF THE PALACE OF THE TOBIADS

The palace, at Araq-el-Emir, Transjordan, near Hesbon, was built by Hyrcanus, a grandson of Tobias, the ancestor of the Tobiads, a very influential dynasty of tax collectors under the Ptolemies and Seleucidae. He called the palace Tyrus and lived there in retirement after his rebellions had failed until his death by suicide in 175/74 B.C.E.

The building shows the blending of the indigenous oriental tradition with Greco-Alexandrian art forms. Giant hewn stones carry a frieze of beasts with figures of lions in high relief. Among the Greek elements of the palace are an acanthus leaf calyx at the foot of the pillar shafts and unconventional forms of Corinthian capitals, while the frieze of lions and bulls' heads goes back to Babylonian and Persian precedent.

SILVER COIN

inscribed "Beka,"[1] "one-half," the designation of a half-shekel (period of
Nehemiah, middle of the 5th century). The pagan character of the coin does
not disprove the assumption that the coin was struck by a Jewish authority.
The seals of earlier centuries and later ones, such as the *Yehud* coins (see
p. 55) show the same reproductions of pagan representations.

The obverse of the coin shows a bearded head which is also found on contemporaneous coins of coastal cities. A stylistic relationship appears to exist
with some of the heads in the Persepolis rock reliefs of the same period.
The head of the woman on the reverse has much in common with the Aphro-
dite represented on the early Greek coins. It also recalls the Palestinian
"pillar Astarte" figurines (see p. 43), though these are of a much cruder
workmanship. *Twice the actual size.*

From the author's collection.

בקע [1

COINS AND WEIGHT

1,2   Coins, inscribed in Hebrew *Yehud*[1] (Judea under Persian rulership 5th and 4th centuries).

It is not certain which deity the portrait in no. 1 represents. The coinage of the Persian satraps portrays the Baal of Tarsus in similar fashion. Zeus holding an eagle in his hand appears in similar attitude upon the coinage of Alexander the Great. Greek influence is apparent in the satyr's head (no. 2) and especially in the head wearing a Corinthian helmet, no. 1, obverse. The same influence is present in the *Yehud* coins which display the owl of Athena (no. 3, reverse). The similarity between these coins and those of the Philistine cities minted at the same time is unmistakable. *1 twice, 2 five times the actual size.*

1, British Museum, 2, Collection of the late Dr. Salzberger, Jerusalem.

3   Coin, inscribed "Hezekiah"[2] (from Beth-zur) ; Hezekiah may have been the high priest and friend of Ptolemy I (323-285) whom we know from Josephus (*Contra Apionem* I: 187-189). *Five times the actual size.*

Rockefeller Museum, Jerusalem.

4   Hebrew weight, tortoise-shaped, inscribed *"Pelag reva,"*[3] "half one-quarter" (of a shekel) ; the form of the weight is due to Babylonian influence. *Twice the original size.*

From the author's collection.

1] יהוד   2] יחזקיה   3] פלג רבע

PAPYRUS FROM ELEPHANTINE

This papyrus, of which only a segment is reproduced,[1] is the copy of a petition which the leader of the Jewish community at Elephantine in Upper Egypt sent to the Persian governor of Judea in 408/07 B.C.E.

The Jewish community at Elephantine, a military colony, suffered persecution and the letter describes how a conspiracy between the Persian governor and the Egyptian priests had led to the destruction of its temple. The leader of the community, Yedoniah, concludes by petitioning the Persian governor of Judea, Bagohi, for the reconstruction of the temple. The letter appears to have followed a previous appeal to the high priest Johanan at Jerusalem that had remained unanswered. (The high priest as well as the Persian governor are known from the Bible: Neh. 7:7, etc.)

A number of letters from the Jewish colony of Elephantine have survived. The dryness of the climate, unlike that of Palestine, protected the papyri from disintegration. The letters, from the 5th and 4th centuries B.C.E., throw light upon the relations between the Diaspora and the high priest of the province of Judea. They contain a wealth of detail about the mercenary Jewish troops which garrisoned the border fortress of Syene and, in a strange land, remained faithful to their God.

1]

אל מראן בגוהי פחת יהוד עבדיך י
מראן אלה שמיא ישאל שגיא בכל
ובני ביתא יתיר מן זי כען חד אלף
כען עבדך ידניה וכנותה כן אמרן
נפק ואזל על מלכא כמריא זי אלהא חנוב זי
הוה לם אגורא זי יהו אלהא זי
לחיא אגרת שלח על נפין ברה זי ר
בירתא ינדשו אחר נפין דבר מצר
עלו באגורה זך נדשוהי עד ארעא
זי אבן 5 בנין פסילה זי אבן זי ה
זי דששיא אלך נחש ומטלל ע
הוה כלא באשה שרפו ומזרקיא זי זה
ולנפשהום עבדו ומן יומי מלך מצרין א
אגורא זך בנה השכחה ואגורי אלה
וכזי כזנה עבדו אנחנה עם נשין ובנין
זי החוין בוידרנג זך כלביא הנפקו כבלא
זי בעו באיש לאגורא זך כל קטילו

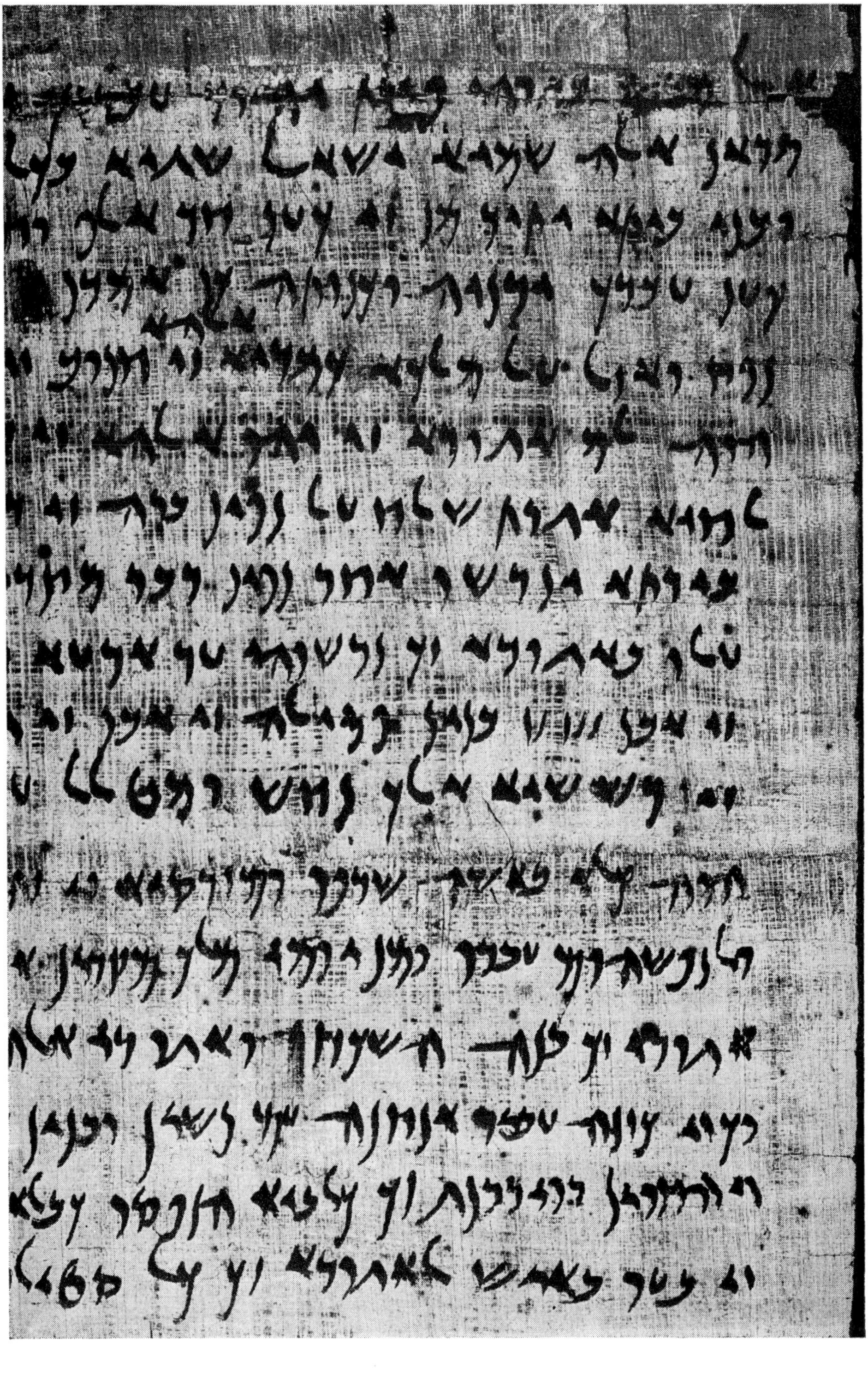

THE MACCABEAN PERIOD

THE "TOMB OF ZACHARIAS"

is one of a group of tomb monuments in the Kidron Valley (Jerusalem).
All of these monuments, the "Hand of Absalom," the "Beth ha-Hofshit" and
the "Tomb of Zacharias" are hewn from the rock and show a peculiar mix-
ture of different styles.
The pyramidal roof and the hollow groove pattern on the frieze of the "Tomb
of Zacharias" derive from Egyptian models, the capitals follow Greek precedent, and Phoenician influences are also apparent. The monument has
also pilasters with quarter columns at the corners, hewn from the rock walls.

THE "TOMB OF JEHOSHAPHAT" IN JERUSALEM

Entrance; to the right, the columns of the "Hand of Absalom" with which it is constructionally connected. The ornamented front is Hellenistic-Jewish work; it shows the fruits of the land (grapes, ethrogs, etc.) and acanthus leaves. The monument is one of the finest examples of Jewish tomb construction in the Maccabean period.

THE JUDGES' TOMB IN JERUSALEM

Entrance; one of the stairways leading to the grave debouches into a fore-court, giving upon the inner room by a rectangular or slightly arched portal. The door could be tightly closed by a stone stop or a stone which was rolled to it.

Interior; the dead were buried in thrust graves (*kukhim*), horizontal gal-leries into which the corpses were thrust. After the corpses had disintegrated the bones were buried in chests (ossuaries; see pp. 64 ff.), and the thrust grave was free for new bodies.

OSSUARIES

THE OSSUARIES in which the bones of the dead were buried were made from wood, clay or limestone. Most of them are from .50 to .80 m long, from .20 to .30 m wide, and from .30 to .40 m high. The lids of the ossuaries were either flat, slightly arched, or gable-shaped. Usually the outside of the bone chests was ornamented. The names of the dead, in Greek or Hebrew, are often found on them. The character of the inscriptions shows that the ossuaries date from the Hellenistic period, some of them from the 1st centuries B.C.E. and C.E. Their style is influenced by the Hellenistic sarcophagus art.

A special guild of craftsmen engaged in the production of ossuaries, as is shown by a list of ossuary workers found in Jerusalem.

1 Ossuary, upper length .58 m, showing a calyx-shaped glass subsequently added to the original decoration consisting of two six-pointed stars.
Hebrew University, Jerusalem.
2 Ossuary, upper length .59 m, bearing the scratched inscription "Jesus, son of Joseph." This inscription indicates approximately how the founder of Christianity would have written his name.
Published by Professor E. L. Sukenik; Archaeological Museum, Jerusalem.

1

2

OSSUARIES

decorated with stars, rosettes and flowers.
Archaeological Museum, Jerusalem.

MEMORIAL TABLET FOR KING UZZIAH

inscribed in biblical Aramaic "Hither were brought the bones of Uzziah, King of Judah. Do not open."[1] King Uzziah (780-740) had died of leprosy (II Chron. 26:23); his grave, therefore, was not in the royal mausoleum. Apparently, when by a shifting of the walls the burial place came to be within the city area, the tomb had to be transferred and the inscription was prepared (1st century B.C.E.-1st century C.E.).

Found by Professor E. L. Sukenik; at the Russian Elona Church on the Mount of Olives, Jerusalem.

———————

לכה התית טמי עוזיה מלך יהודה ולא למפתח [1]

COINS OF THE
MACCABEAN PERIOD

HE MACCABEAN mintage, while rather unpretentious, is quite characteristic and entirely different from that of neighboring peoples. No representations of God or the heads of rulers appear on these coins. The script, exclusively Hebrew at first, is archaic and resembles writing known from documents of the time of the Kings. This is unquestionably a deliberate nationalist demonstration, for the Aramaic language and square script had long ago displaced the old Hebrew language and writing.

COIN STRUCK BY JOHN HYRCANUS (135-104)

Obv.: Wreath of laurel, inscribed "Jehochanan the High Priest and the Community of the Jews";[1] rv.: double cornucopias, in the center of a poppy head.

יהוחנן הכהן הגדל וחבר היהודים [1]

The mintage of John Hyrcanus and his successors usually shows two cornucopias on the obverse and on the reverse the inscription "Johanan [or Judah or Jonathan] the High Priest and the Community of the Jews." The lettering recalls in its fineness and precision the high quality of the old seal engravers' art.

New types of coins do not appear before Alexander Jannai (Hebrew: Jonathan), the first Hasmonean to place the title of king on the coins struck by him.

1   2

COINS STRUCK BY ALEXANDER JANNAI (103-76)

1   Obv.: Anchor, inscribed in Greek "King Alexander"; rv.: Sun-wheel, inscribed in Hebrew "Jonathan the King."[1]

2   Obv.: Half-opened flower, inscribed in Hebrew "Jonathan the King";[1] rv.: Anchor within broad circle, inscribed in Greek "King Alexander."

1] יהונתן המלך

The inscription is now, in some instances, in Hebrew and Greek. The flowers and anchors of this king are embossed probably on the model of similar Seleucid coins; the anchor possibly refers to the conquest of the coastal towns Jaffa, Gaza, and Raphia. There now also appears for the first time a wheel-like emblem on the coins which is found in later synagogue art; it may be related to the wheels of the chariot in the vision of Ezekiel.

COIN STRUCK BY ANTIGONOS MATTATHIAS (40-37)

Rv.: The seven-branched candlestick, inscribed in Greek "King Ant [igonos]."

The mintage of Antigonos Mattathias, last of the Maccabean rulers, is as such quite insignificant, the coins, contrary to those of earlier times, being made of very base metal. This debasing of the coinage is undoubtedly due to the pillaging of Palestine by the Romans and Parthians. Significant, however, is the appearance now for the first time upon a few coins of the Menorah, the seven-branched candlestick later to become the symbol of Judaism. Its shape generally corresponds to the descriptions of the candlestick in the Tabernacle and to the Temple candlestick carried in the triumphal procession depicted on the Arch of Titus (pp. 78 f.).

All coins from the author's collection.

THE HERODIAN PERIOD

THE TEMPLE OF HEROD

THE RECONSTRUCTION of the Temple was Herod's (37-4 B.C.E.) most important achievement. Josephus (*The Jewish War* V.5, 1) gives the following account: "The temple . . . was built upon a strong hill. At first the plain at the top was hardly sufficient for the holy house and the altar; for the ground about it was very uneven, and like a precipice; but when King Solomon, who was the person that built the temple, had built a wall to it, on its east side, there was then added one cloister founded on a bank cast up for it, and on the other parts the holy house stood naked. But in future ages the people added new banks, and the hill became a larger plain. They then broke down the wall on the north side, and took in as much as sufficed afterward for the compass of the entire temple. And when they had built walls on three sides of the temple round about, from the bottom of the hill, and had performed a work that was greater than could be hoped for (in which work long ages were spent by them, as well as all their sacred treasures were exhausted, which were still replenished by those tributes which were sent to God from the whole habitable earth), they then encompassed their upper courts with cloisters, as well as they [afterward] did the lowest [court of the] temple. The lowest part of this was erected to the height of three hundred cubits, and in some places more; yet did not the entire depth of the foundations appear;

for they brought earth, and filled up the valleys, as being desirous to make them on a level with the narrow streets of the city, wherein they made use of stones of forty cubits in magnitude; for the great plenty of money they then had, and the liberality of the people, made this attempt of theirs to succeed to an incredible degree. And what could not be so much as hoped for as ever to be accomplished, was, by perseverance and length of time, brought to perfection."

Josephus further describes the richness of the material. Cedar and marble were freely used and the doors encased in gold, silver and bronze.

THE WAILING WALL

The Temple of Herod was never completed. Herod began work on it when his reign was in its eighteenth year (20-19 B.C.E.). The construction continued for a long while beyond Herod's lifetime. The temple was destroyed in 70 C.E. Today there exists of all its splendor only the remains of the wall around the Temple square, known as the Wailing Wall.

The huge stones in the foreground are Herodian; not all of them are embossed. The largest of these stones is over five meters long.

1

2

HERODIAN ARCHITECTURE

1   Remains of the temple of Augustus at Sebaste, the new town which
Herod the Great (37-4 B.C.E.) had built on the site of the ancient Samaria
and called Sebaste (the Greek equivalent of the Latin "Augustus") in honor
of his imperial protector.

Herod was a great city builder. Cities such as Phasaelis and Antipatris were
built at his initiative and named after his friends and relatives. Parts of the
walls of Jerusalem built by him (see p. 75) may be seen to this day.

2   Port construction at Caesarea of which the foundations are from the
time of Herod.

FROM THE ARCH OF TITUS IN ROME

The arch was erected in 94 under the Emperor Domitian by the Roman
Senate and people in honor of Emperor Titus. It portrays Titus' triumphal
procession upon his return to Rome after the conquest of Jerusalem and the
destruction of the Temple.

Two leaders of the Jewish war against Rome, Johanan of Gischala and
Simon bar Giora, had been taken to Rome by Titus for his procession, as
well as 700 selected Jewish captives. The spoils of the Temple were publicly
placed on view; their representation upon the relief of the Arch of Titus is
in accordance with Josephus' description.

In front was carried the golden table of the showbread upon which two cups
had been placed. Fastened to it are two Temple trumpets, exactly as they
are found later on the coins of Bar Kokhba. The Menorah, the seven-
branched candlestick, follows; its pedestal may be a free rendering by a
Roman artist.

Picture on pp. 78 f.

1

FROM THE TEMPLE OF HEROD

1   Greek inscription: "No alien may enter within the balustrade and the enclosure around the sanctuary. Whoever is caught, on himself shall be put blame for the death which will ensue."

This is one of the two warning inscriptions of Herod's temple which have been found. Placed on the balustrade before the Holy Place of the Temple they warned the pagan visitor not to proceed and thus commit an act of desecration. Execution by the outraged community would be the fate of the violator. In compliance with Jewish law the tablets forewarned the trespasser of the consequences.

At the Istanbul Museum.

2   Stamp, inscribed "Eleazar A[lpha]";[1] according to the Mishnah only the "Alpha," the best quality of flour, oil and wine were used for the temple offerings; this stamp, with dealer Eleazar's guarantee for "Alpha" quality, was probably used to seal jars containing the wine for the temple offerings. From the author's collection.

אלע[1]

זרA

2

GREEK INSCRIPTION FROM A SYNAGOGUE

which was found on a limestone block at the Ophel and dates from the century preceding the destruction of the Second (Herodian) Temple. It reads: "Theodotos, son of Vettenos, priest and archisynagogos, son of an archisynagogos, grandson of an archisynagogos, built the synagogue for the reading of the law and for the teaching of the commandments; furthermore the hospice and the chambers, and the water installation, for the lodging of needy strangers. The foundation stone thereof had been laid by his fathers, and the elders, and Simonides."

The inscription proves that the "synagogue" which was to take the place of the temple had already begun to exercise its influence before the Temple ceased to exist. Possibly the synagogue built by Theodotos is identical with the "synagogue of the Libertines," mentioned in Acts 6:9.

Excavated by R. Weill on behalf of Baron E. de Rothschild; now at the Archaeological Museum, Jerusalem.

COINS OF THE HERODIANS (37 B.C.E.-100 C.E.)

1   Coin struck by Herod the Great (37-4 B.C.E.), showing ritual objects, a censer and a tripod.

2   Coin struck by Herod the Great, showing an anchor and cornucopias.

3   Coin struck by Herod the Great, showing an eagle; it recalls the golden eagle upon the Temple of Jerusalem; generally, however, the mintings of Herod avoided representations of living beings.

4   Coin struck by Herod Philippus (4 B.C.E.-34 C.E.), showing the temple, built by Herod in honor of Augustus, and Caesar's portrait.

5   Coin struck at Tiberias by Herod Antipas (4 B.C.E.-39 C.E.), showing a palm branch.

6   Coin struck by Archelaus (4 B.C.E.-6 C.E.), showing a helmet and a bunch of grapes; the latter is a motif which occurs frequently in later synagogue art.

All coins in actual size.

From the author's collection.

COINS OF THE HERODIANS

1   Portrait coin, struck at Caesarea by Agrippa I (37-44). This coin refers to the gladiatorial games held in Caesar's honor; the reverse shows a figure holding rudder and palm branch, symbols of the games.

2   Coin struck by Agrippa I, showing ears of barley.

3   Portrait coin of King Herod of Chalcis (41-48), a brother of Agrippa I.

4   Portrait coin of Aristobulus of Chalcis (70-92), son of Herod of Chalcis; on the reverse, portrait of his wife, Salome.

5   Portrait coin of Aristobulus of Chalcis.

6   Portrait coin of Agrippa II (50-100) as a youth.

7,8   Coins struck by Agrippa II, showing portraits of the reigning Roman emperor, done entirely in Roman-Hellenistic style.

All coins in actual size, excepting no. 2 (enlarged).

1, 2, 7 and 8 from the author's collection; 3, 4 and 5 Coin Cabinet of the Bibliothèque Nationale, Paris; 6 Coin Cabinet, Munich.

THE PERIOD OF THE
REVOLTS AGAINST ROME

COINS OF THE PROCURATORS AND
ROMAN VICTORY COINS (44-98)

1-5   Coins of the Roman procurators (44-66) showing among other motifs the augur's staff, shield and spear; out of consideration for the feelings of the Jewish people no portraits were used.

6   Roman victory coin, in commemoration of the conquest of Judea (67-70), inscribed *Judaea Capta*, showing a mourning Jewess to the left and a captive Jew to the right of a palm tree, the symbol of Judea.

7   Roman victory coin, inscribed *Judaea*, showing a mourning Jewess and a trophy.

8   Coin struck by Nerva (96-98), showing a palm tree and the inscription *Fisci Judaici Calumnia Sublata*, "the insult of the Jewish tax was removed": this refers to the yearly levy for the temple of Jupiter Capitolinus in Rome which had replaced the Temple tax.

All coins in actual size.

1-6, from the author's collection; 7 and 8, Museum of the Hebrew University, Jerusalem.

COINS OF THE JEWISH WAR (66-70)

Bronze box (pyxis) filled with Tyrian shekels and shekels of the Jewish War. Buried in Jerusalem in 67 C.E. and recently recovered, it contains Hebrew coins dated with the years of the rebellion against the Roman overlords.

The representations on the coins are specifically Jewish. Nothing of this sort was minted by the Hellenistic towns in Palestine, which followed the tenets of Hellenistic-Roman culture; the people at large held to Jewish tradition.

From the author's collection.

COINS OF THE JEWISH WAR (66-70 C.E.)

1   Bronze coin, obv.: narrow-necked amphora, inscribed "Year Two"[1] (67/8); rv.: vine branch with leaf and tendril, inscribed "Deliverance of Zion."[2]

2   Silver half-shekel, obv.: chalice with knob on stem and cover, inscribed "Half-shekel Year 3"[3] (68/9); rv.: stem with bunch of three pomegranates, inscribed "Jerusalem the Holy."[4]

3   Silver shekel, obv.: chalice with knob on stem and cover, inscribed "Shekel of Israel Year 3"[5]; rv.: stem with bunch of three pomegranates, inscribed "Jerusalem the Holy."[4]

4   Obv.: lulav between two ethrogs, inscribed "Year Four"[6] (69/70); rv.: chalice with knob on stem and cover, inscribed in retrograde "For the Redemption of Zion."[7]

5   Obv.: ethrog between two lulavs, inscribed "Year Four-One half";[8] rv.: palm tree between two baskets filled with fruit, inscribed "For the Redemption of Zion."[7]

Actual sizes.

From the author's collection.

5| שקל   4| ירושלים הקדושה   3| חצי שקל שג   2| חרות ציון   1| שנת שתים

שג ישראל   6| שנת ארבע   7| לגאלת ציון   8| שנת ארבע חצי

THE ROCK FORTRESS OF MASADA

At Masada, on the western shore of the Dead Sea, the "Jewish War" ended.
The rock was first fortified during the Maccabean wars. Later its fortifica-
tions were enlarged by Herod.

Toward the end of the war against the Romans, Zealot forces led by Eleazar
ben Yair held the fortress. It was well provided with food and arms and
refused to surrender. Silva, the new governor of Palestine and Syria, com-
manded the numerous Roman assault troops. He surrounded Masada with
dams and walls and placed upon them battering rams and ballistas. The
Romans succeeded in breaching the fortress walls only to find a second inner
wall, strongly padded, which the Jews had hurriedly built. Eventually un-
able to take the fortress by direct assault the Romans destroyed it by incendi-
aries. When they entered the gutted fortress they found that the besieged
men, women and children had preferred death by their own hands to cap-
tivity.

In the picture of Masada today, the remains of the circular wall are to be
seen, as are at the far (northern) end the depots and their towers. On the
plateau, to the left, near the wall, is the palace of Herod. Farther left, down
the rock, the dam which the Romans built to move up their assault machines
(a white spot) and remains of the Roman camp are visible. The remnants
of the Roman blockade wall may be seen in the valley.

COINS OF THE BAR KOKHBA REVOLT (132-135)

The coins of Bar Kokhba exemplify the anti-Roman character of his movement. They emphasize Jewish tradition, show again the old emblems and
express in new symbols the national ideals.

1   Silver coin, tetradrachm, the equivalent of the shekel, showing lulav and
ethrog (obv.), and the front of a synagogue with a Torah shrine containing
two scrolls of the law (rv.); inscribed "Second Year of the Freedom of
Israel"[1] [133] (obv.), "Jerusalem"[2] (rv.).

2   Bronze coin, showing palm tree (obv.) and vine leaf (rv.); inscribed
"Simon"[3] (obv.), "For the Freedom of Jerusalem"[4] (rv.).

3   Denarius, showing bunch of grapes (obv.); inscribed "Eleazar the
Priest"[5] (obv.), "Simon"[3] (rv.)

4   Denarius, showing lyre (obv.) and bunch of grapes (rv.); inscribed
"Second Year of the Freedom of Israel"[1] (obv.) "Simon"[3] (rv.)

5   Bronze coin, showing palm tree (obv.) and bunch of grapes (rv.); inscribed "Eleazar the Priest"[5] (retrograde) (obv.), "First Year of the Redemption of Israel"[6] (rv.).

6   Denarius, showing two trumpets with a pellet between; inscribed "For
the Freedom of Jerusalem."[4]

7   Bronze coin, showing lyre (cithara) with three strings; inscribed
"Simon."[3]

8   Bronze coin, showing amphora (obv.); inscribed "First Year of the Redemption of Israel"[7] (obv.) "Simon Nasi Israel"[8] (rv.).

9   Denarius of Trajan, overstamped by Bar Kokhba's followers.

Actual sizes, with exception of no. 9, which is twice the actual size.
From the author's collection.

אלעזר ‏[5   לחרות ירושלם ‏[4   שמעון ‏[3   ירו שלם ‏[2   ש ב לחר ישראל ‏[1

שמעון ‏[8   שנת אחת ולג‏[א‏]לת ישראל ‏[7   שנת אחת לגאלת ישר‏[א‏]ל ‏[6   הכהן
נשיא ישראל

1

2

3

4

5

6

7

9

8a

8b

THE ROMAN PERIOD

PALESTINIAN SYNAGOGUES

AFTER the bloody suppression by Rome (135 C.E.) of the rebellion of Bar Kokhba, Judea was greatly devastated. Galilee, which had been spared the horrors of the war, became the center of Jewish cultural life. Only at the end of the 3rd century did Judea begin to live again. It was in this period, the 3rd and 4th centuries C.E., that places of worship sprang up throughout the country. Of these synagogues only ruins remained.

These synagogues present a new style of place of worship: the basilica. The basilica-type synagogue arose in answer to the need for space in which to carry out the new conception of a sacrificeless worship; and also from the trend to incorporate the established traditional architectural forms. Thus pagan forms of Roman basilica architecture were adapted for the first time to the needs of a non-pagan community. The synagogue basilica became the prototype of the Christian basilica buildings, and only indirectly can the Roman basilica be considered the model of the Christian basilica.

The Palestinian synagogues were not only places of worship but at the same time community houses in the widest sense. Schoolrooms and guest chambers are often found connected with them. Generally, the Palestinian basilica synagogue of the Roman period was entered through a spacious forecourt. It consisted of a room divided by two rows of pillars into a nave and two aisles. These two rows of pillars were joined by a further row at the side opposite the entrance. At the side where the entrance lay, such a connecting row of pillars is never found, which shows that special emphasis was laid upon the entrance. For originally almost without exception the entrance and the front oriented toward Jerusalem; in Galilee toward the south, in Transjordan toward the west. This stressing of the entrance, facing Jerusalem, also corresponds with the rich architecture of the façade and the great window placed there. Here, in the front, was placed the Torah shrine, in early times movable and without any set place. Therefore the congregation stood turned toward the entrance, facing the Torah shrine.

In later times, when the Torah shrine had its fixed place, it was built into the side opposite the entrance, and so changed the whole arrangement. In the later synagogues the entrance was thus on the side away from Jerusalem, while the niche with the Torah shrine was faced toward Jerusalem.

The niche with the Torah shrine parallels the niches for the gods in pagan temples; and the oriented Torah niche becomes the Christian apse in which the altar was set. Just as the apse of the basilica-type synagogue held the Torah, so the Christian apse represented the most sacred space in the church.

RUINS OF THE SYNAGOGUE AT KFAR BIRIM, UPPER GALILEE

The synagogue stood on a mountain top; its remains consist of the façade with three entrances and part of the portico.

Excavated by the Palestine Exploration Fund and the Deutsche Orient Gesellschaft.

THE SYNAGOGUE OF CAPERNAUM ON
LAKE TIBERIAS

Reconstruction, according to Kohl and Watzinger; three doors of the two-storied building which measured 20.4 m x 18.65 m, led into the synagogue court, an outside stairway to the gallery; the synagogue had a slanting brick roof and a "Syrian" pediment.

Ruins of the synagogue; part of it was rebuilt by the Franciscan order in 1925, sixty years after C. W. Wilson uncovered a portion of the ruins. Excavated by the Deutsche Orient Gesellschaft and the Custodia della Terra Santa.

FROM THE SYNAGOGUE AT CAPERNAUM

1 Stone ornament; hexagram, pomegranates and sunwheel, typical decoration of the torus frieze on the entablature which served to enliven the straight lines of the superstructure; similar ornaments appear earlier in a similarly rigid manner upon Maccabean tomb façades, on coins and ossuaries.

2 Ark of the Covenant, conceived as a movable Torah shrine, about .33 m high; a movable Ark of the Covenant also appears in the frescos at Dura Europos (p. 126).

3 Pillar capital with the seven-branched candlestick, shofar and censer, about .7 m.

Excavated by the Deutsche Orient Gesellschaft and the Custodia della Terra Santa.

RUINS OF THE SYNAGOGUE AT ESHTEMOA

Eshtemoa was a little village, about three and one-half miles south of Yatta in the Hebron district. The synagogue (4th century) which measured 13.33 m x 21.3 m stood at its most elevated site; the western wall, in the center of the picture, is about ten yards high; the building in the background dates from the period of the Crusades.

TORAH NICHE OF THE SYNAGOGUE AT ESHTEMOA

The niche, 1.73 m wide, .86 m deep, opened into a rectangle, 2.11 m wide and .73 m deep; its total depth was almost 1.6 m. It was placed 2.08 m above the floor and flanked on both sides by small niches. This arrangement recalls numerous Roman buildings in Syria, Palestine, and Transjordan, where the main entrance gate is flanked by niches, sometimes in two rows, at other times in a single row above small doors. The ancient Jewish carving reproduced p. 100, no. 3 suggests that seven-branched candlesticks were placed in the small niches; the middle niche served as a Torah shrine facing north as Eshtemoa is south of Jerusalem.

Excavated by L. A. Mayer and A. Reifenberg.

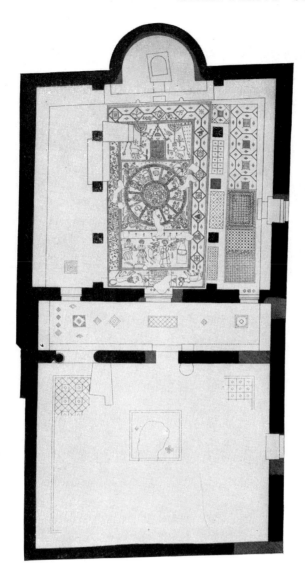

GROUND PLAN OF THE SYNAGOGUE AT
BETH ALPHA

The total length of the structure, a basilica divided by two rows of columns into a main nave and two side aisles, was 27.7 m; excluding the adjoining chambers its width was 14.2 m. The synagogue at Beth Alpha is distinguished from other Palestinian synagogues by an apse and *bemah* the remains of which were found.

Excavated by the Hebrew University, Jerusalem.

STONE ORNAMENTS FROM SYNAGOGUES

1 Head of Medusa (from the synagogue of Chorazin).
2 Frieze with amphorae and sunwheel (from synagogue of Eshtemoa).

1

FROM
SYNAGOGUES

1   Chair of the "Archisynagogos," the head of the elders of the synagogue, from the synagogue at Chorazin (Kerazeh, north of Capernaum), .56 m high, .73 m wide, .565 m maximum thickness. This kind of chair, the "Chair of Moses," known from Jewish literature and the New Testament, was placed on the raised *bemah*, the dais from which the Torah was read. The inscription at the frontside of the chair reads: "Remembered be for good Judan b. Ishmael who made this stoa and its staircase. As his reward may he have a share with the righteous."[1]
Excavated by the Deutsche Orient Gesellschaft and the Department of Antiquities, British Mandatory Government of Palestine.
2   Representation of the zodiac, from the synagogue at Kfar Birim (N.W. of Safed in Galilee).
Excavated by the Deutsche Orient Gesellschaft and the Department of Antiquities, British Mandatory Government of Palestine.

1] דכיר לטב יודן בר ישמעאל דעבד הדן סטוה ודרגוה בפעלה יהי לה חולק עם
צדיקים

2

1

2

DETAIL FROM SYNAGOGUES

1　Marble screen, about .18 m high, showing candlestick, shofar, lulav, and ethrog (from the synagogue at Ascalon). The screen separated the Torah shrine from the rest of the building. In the same way in Christian churches the apsidal space was shut off from the public by the chancel screen.

At the German Evangelic Palestine Institute, Jerusalem.

2　Lintel, 1.98 m long, showing the seven-branched candlestick, a Torah scroll (?), a cup, and scallop shells (from a synagogue in Nave).

THE HOUSES OF NAVE

The basalt houses of Naua in Hauran, the ancient Jewish Nave, standing to
this day and now occupied by Arabs, are an instructive example of Jewish
architecture in Roman times.

Private two-storied residence, with lintel showing a wreath, grape ornaments
and amphorae.

HOUSE IN NAVE

Private residence with lintel showing a shell within a wreath, plant ornaments, and two seven-branched candlesticks; the interior is shown on the
next page.

INTERIOR OF
HOUSE IN NAVE

Stone ornament from a
house in Nave, showing
the seven-branched
candlestick, censer,
lulav, and grapes.

ENTRANCE TO A HOUSE IN NAVE

This house, probably a synagogue, contains, high up in the wall facing Jerusalem, a niche which served to hold the Torah scrolls. Like the majority of the houses in Roman Hauran, it is constructed as a "broad-house."

SYNAGOGUE MOSAICS

MOSAIC PAVEMENTS are preserved in many synagogues of Palestine and the Diaspora. In a few places, such as Kafr Kenna and Sepphoris, the only decorations are the inscriptions of names of the builders or donors; other mosaics are adorned with pictorial representations.

The Palestinian Talmud alludes in a passage to the use of pictorial representations: "In the days of Rabbi Abun [4th century] they began to display paintings on mosaics, and he did not prevent them." Even the mythological imagery of the neighbors of the Jewish people appears in the mosaics. Hellenistic influence is evident in the adoption of many pagan symbols. Thus the allusion is to the image of the sun god in his chariot when Midrash *Pirke de Rabbi Eliezer* says: "The sun rides in a chariot and rises crowned as a bridegroom." But these adopted themes usually assume in the Jewish world of ideas a special symbolic significance.

An iconoclastic movement in later times resulted in the destruction of most of the synagogue mosaics. Preserved were the pictorial representations of synagogues which were destroyed by earthquakes, such as Beth Alpha, or were allowed to fall into disuse, like Chorazin in the 4th or Gerasa in the 5th century.

MOSAIC PAVEMENT FROM THE SYNAGOGUE OF AEGINA, GREECE

It is composed of blue, gray, red and black stones and gives the effect of a carpet. The Greek inscription names "Theodoros," an elder of the synagogue.

Excavated by the German Archaeological Institute.

MOSAIC FROM THE SYNAGOGUE AT
ESFIYA ON MT. CARMEL

showing a seven-branched candlestick with censer and shofar (left), ethrog
and lulav (right), 1 m long and .8 m wide.
Excavated by the Department of Antiquities, British Mandatory Government of Palestine.

DETAIL OF THE MOSAIC FROM THE SYNAGOGUE

AT ESFIYA ON MT. CARMEL

showing one of the four seasons, part of the representation of the zodiac, about .5 x .5 m.

The representation of the zodiac in a synagogue (see also p. 105, no. 2, stone carvings from Kfar Birim, and p. 118, mosaic from the synagogue at Beth Alpha) seems surprising. But Josephus already connected the twelve show-bread of the Temple, and Philo the twelve precious stones on the high priest's breastplate, with the twelve signs of the zodiac. Rabbi Hanina declared that in his opinion the constellation under which a man is born determines his destiny. The *Sepher Yetzirah* (Book of Creation), composed probably between the 3rd and 6th centuries, gives for the first time a complete enumeration of the constellations; in the 7th century it is found in the liturgical poetry of Kalir.

Excavated by the Department of Antiquities, British Mandatory Government of Palestine.

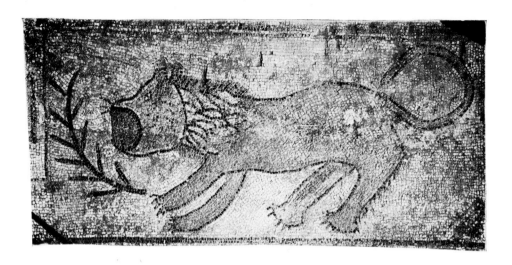

MOSAIC FROM THE SYNAGOGUE AT BETH ALPHA

(6TH CENTURY)

showing a lion and an ox, flanking a dated inscription in Aramaic and Greek
(not shown here), part of a border, from .6 to .9 m wide. The entire floor
of the synagogue is laid in a mosaic with amazingly primitive representations.

Excavated by the Hebrew University, Jerusalem.

MOSAIC FROM THE SYNAGOGUE AT BETH ALPHA

(6TH CENTURY)

Section, showing the sacrifice of Isaac: the sacrificial altar, Isaac and Abraham (right), the hand of God and the ram (center), the waiting servants and the donkey (left), and the following inscriptions: above the ram, "And behold a ram"[1] (Gen. 22:13); above the branch symbolizing the thicket, "Lay not[2] [thy hand]" (Gen. 22:12); above Abraham's head, "Abraham";[3] above Isaac's head, "Isaac."[4]

Excavated by the Hebrew University, Jerusalem.

1] והנה איל   2] אל תשלח   3] אברהם   4] יצחק

MOSAIC FROM THE SYNAGOGUE AT BETH ALPHA

(6TH CENTURY)

Section, next to the Torah shrine of the synagogue, showing a shrine flanked by two birds above and two lions below, two seven-branched candlesticks, twofold descriptions of lulav, ethrog and shofar, and a censer. The curtain is pictured as drawn back before the shrine.

Lions are very often represented in mosaics. Flanking the Torah shrine they appear to be a derivation from the biblical cherubim and also an allusion to the tribe of Judah guarding the holy law, the lion being the heraldic beast of Judah.

Excavated by the Hebrew University, Jerusalem.

MOSAIC FROM THE SYNAGOGUE AT BETH ALPHA
(6TH CENTURY)

showing in the center piece Phoebus in his horse-drawn chariot, surrounded by the moon and the stars, in the outer circle the zodiac explained by Hebrew inscriptions, and in the corners winged genii symbolizing the four seasons in accordance with Roman art (see p. 114 concerning the use of the zodiac in synagogue art). The diameter of the outer circle is 3.12 m, contained within a square measuring 3.55 x 3.75 m.

Excavated by the Hebrew University, Jerusalem.

MOSAIC FROM THE SYNAGOGUE AT EL-HAMMEH

(4TH TO FIRST HALF OF 5TH CENTURY)

The Aramaic inscription, which mentions several Jews as benefactors of the synagogue, reads:

"And remembered be for good Kyris Hoples, and Kyra Protone, and Kyris Sallustius his son-in-law, and Comes Phroros his son, and Kyris Photios his son-in-law, and Kyris Haninah his son — they and their children — whose acts of charity are constant everywhere [and] who have given here five denarii [of] gold. May the King of the Universe bestow the blessing upon their work. Amen. Amen. Selah."

Excavated by the Hebrew University, Jerusalem.

THE FRESCOS FROM THE
SYNAGOGUE OF DURA EUROPOS

THE INTERIOR DECORATION of the synagogue was very often magnificent. The most remarkable find in the field of synagogue art are the frescos found 1932 to 1935 in the synagogue of Dura Europos, a Syrian caravan city on the Euphrates. The synagogue dates from the year 245 C.E. Pagan temples and a Christian church, built by converting a private home, were uncovered near by.

Babylonian Jewry, through centuries of relative quiet, had reached a singularly high social and cultural level. Under the Exilarchs, they were loyal to their religious and cultural traditions. In the 3rd century C.E. the Babylonian communities experienced a remarkable flowering when the academies of Sura and Nehardea were founded after the pattern of the Palestinian academies.

In the Syrian border town of Dura Europos there resided also many Jews of Hellenistic culture who had come from such Diaspora centers as Antioch and Alexandria. Thus while the Jewish population of Dura Europos upheld Jewish traditions, it received numerous influences from the Syro-Hellenistic world, and also, due to the town's character as a caravan city, from Mesopotamia.

The frescos of the synagogue exhibit dramatic scenes from biblical history: Moses before the burning bush; Joshua with the angel who appears before him prior to the fall of Jericho; the miracle of the Amorite war, when at Joshua's bidding the sun and moon stood still in their course. Also shown are Moses leading the Hebrews out of Egypt, the Egyptians drowning in the waters, David playing the harp, the sacrifice of Elijah upon Carmel, the vision of Ezekiel; and other subjects. The pictures are explained in part by inscriptions in Aramaic, Greek and Pehlevi, the Persian language in use from the 3rd to the 7th centuries.

Characteristic of the synagogue frescos is the pictorial concentration on the story element. The Christian frescos discovered at Dura have almost everything of style and composition in common with the pagan paintings also found at Dura, with the one exception that the Christian, like the Jewish frescos, lay strong emphasis upon the depiction of the story detail, often at the expense of artistic expression. Hence it is believed that Christendom adopted this kind of representation from Judaism and that the specifically Christian style noted for such emphasis was developed in the East and not in Rome.

Excavated by Yale University; the synagogue frescos were transferred to the National Museum in Damascus and included in a reconstruction of the synagogue.

PHARAOH WITH HIS DAUGHTER AND MOSES' MOTHER

FROM THE SYNAGOGUE AT DURA EUROPOS

Torah niche and above it fresco showing a building similar to the Temple (synagogue) with a Torah shrine flanked by a seven-branched candlestick, lulav and ethrog (left) and the sacrifice of Isaac (right); Abraham is preparing to proceed with the sacrifice of his son who lies upon the altar, when the hand of God appears (above the altar); below, tied to a tree is seen the ram which is to be the sacrifice in place of Isaac.

The composition of the Torah shrine emphatically recalls the representation of Torah shrines on coins of the Bar Kokhba revolt (p. 92).

FRESCO FROM THE SYNAGOGUE AT
DURA EUROPOS

Moses striking water from the rock; the water flows in twelve streams to the twelve tents before the Tabernacle, the encampment of the twelve tribes of Israel.

ONE OF THE SONS OF AARON

JOSHUA

FRESCOS FROM THE SYNAGOGUE AT DURA EUROPOS

The return of the Ark of the Covenant from the hands of the Philistines (I Sam. 6); the five persons represented are probably the five princes of the Philistines, the devastation the Ark has wrought in the Philistine camp is seen in the temple of Dagon (top right): the idols are thrown down from their pedestals, the debris lies strewn upon the ground among broken cult vessels and musical instruments.

Presumably Jeremiah holding in his hands a Torah scroll; the Egypto-Alex-
andrian influence is especially noticeable if the face is compared with
mummy-portraits of the 2nd century.

HAMAN AND MORDECAI

THE ART OF THE CATACOMBS

FROM 1936 TO 1940 excavations were undertaken at Beth-shearim, the city which, situated at the entrance to the valley of Jezreel (the Emek), was the temporary seat of the Sanhedrin in the 2nd century C.E. Most important of the excavated monuments are, besides the synagogue which also served as a court room, the eleven catacombs, all similar in arrangement. It appears that the bodies of Jews from Asia Minor, Palmyra, Arabia and other faraway places were brought for burial to Beth-shearim.

The custom of burial in catacombs was not confined to Palestine. There were Jewish catacombs in the 1st century C.E. in nearly all the countries of the Jewish Diaspora, in Italy, North Africa, and many islands of the Mediterranean. The most interesting of these are the catacombs of Rome. Sporadically, sarcophagi occur in Roman catacombs.

CATACOMB AT BETH-SHEARIM

A passage hewn in the rock forms the entrance to a burial hall which can be
closed with a stone door. The burial halls were situated upon either side of
the catacomb. Above the entrance are inscriptions, carved or painted, mostly
in Greek, some in Hebrew, Aramaic, or Palmyrene. They usually give the
name of the head of the family.

The resting place of the dead consisted of an arcosolium, an arched tomb
which on the narrow side had a raised part for the head of the dead.

Excavated by the Jewish Palestine Exploration Society.

A BURIAL HALL, CATACOMB AT BETH-SHEARIM

Most of the burial halls have several chambers separated from each other
by arches resting on pillars. The walls of the tomb chambers are decorated
with reliefs, drawings, and inscriptions, among which the seven-branched
candlestick is the most common theme.

Excavated by the Jewish Palestine Exploration Society.

1

CATACOMB AT BETH-SHEARIM

1 Wall picture of a man and his horse.
2 Chamber of the Palmyrene Jews, with wall decorations, a candlestick, a Palmyrene inscription on the archway, and a representation of a Torah shrine in the background.
Excavated by the Jewish Palestine Exploration Society.

2

CATACOMB AT BETH-SHEARIM

Primitive representation of a man bearing a candlestick upon his head.
Excavated by the Jewish Palestine Exploration Society.

FROM THE CATACOMB AT MONTE VERDE, ROME
(1ST TO 4TH CENTURIES)

1   Greek tomb inscription, "Eulogia," 4th century, marble, .225 m high, .455 m wide, .02 m thick, showing an open Torah shrine with Torah scrolls, flanked by a seven-branched and a five-branched candlestick.

2   Greek tomb inscription, "Donatos, secretary of the synagogue of the Vernaculi," 2nd or 3rd century, .31 m high, .44 m wide, .03 m thick, showing candlesticks, ethrog, oil jar, and lulav.

Museo Nazionale, Naples.

FRESCO FROM THE CATACOMB AT THE
VILLA TORLONIA IN ROME

The fresco, part of a wall-painting, which covers an ark in the catacomb, shows a seven-branched candlestick.

FRESCOS FROM THE CATACOMB OF THE

VILLA TORLONIA IN ROME

on p. 135.

Torah scroll (1) and pomegranate (2) which flank the candlestick shown

FRESCOS FROM THE CATACOMB OF THE
VILLA TORLONIA IN ROME

1 Torah shrine between two candlesticks; over it arches the firmament
with sun, moon and a star; ethrog and circumcision knife (right), palm
branch and pomegranate (left); a bottle in red, probably sacred Sabbath
wine, between the candlestick on the left and the shrine. The star may signify
a symbol of messianic hope.

2 Dolphin and trident.

MARBLE SARCOPHAGUS FROM THE
VILLA RANDANINI IN ROME

A fragment, .72 m high, 1.26 m long, probably the work of a pagan sculptor for a Jew, showing a round shield (clipeus) with a seven-branched candlestick upheld by two genii; beneath the candlestick, three boys treading grapes, to the right, representations of the seasons of summer and winter. At the Museo Nazionale, Rome.

STONE CARVING FROM TIBERIAS

showing the seven-branched candlestick, lulav and shofar; .38 x .48 m, 3rd
to 5th centuries.
Musée du Louvre, Paris.

BONE CARVING FROM BETH-SHAN

showing the seven-branched candlestick with lulav, shofar and ethrog (left)
and incense shovel (right), .096m long, 3rd to 6th centuries.
Department of Antiquities, British Mandatory Government of Palestine.

MARBLE RELIEF FROM PRIENE, ASIA MINOR

showing the seven-branched candlestick with ethrog, lulav and shofar, .615
m high, 3rd to 4th century; the rolls at the base of the candlestick have
been interpreted as Torah scrolls.
Kaiser Friedrich Museum, Berlin.

1

2

STAMPS

Stamps for the sealing of property were in general use in antiquity. Among the Jews the same custom prevailed, especially for the purpose of certifying food as prepared according to ritual regulations. The following stamps date from the third to fifth centuries.

1   Bronze stamp, with a broad ring on its back, showing the seven-branched candlestick, shofar and lulav (from Antioch, Syria).
From the author's collection.

2   Stamp, showing a candlestick, cluster of grapes and palm branch, inscribed "Leontiou" (from Sardes, Lydia, Asia Minor). The grapes possibly indicate that the stamp was used for wine jars. British Museum, London.

3   Bronze stamp, showing the candlestick and its attributes, inscribed "Theodora." Museo Nazionale, Rome.
All stamps actual size.

3

1

2

AMULETS

1   Hebrew ring-stone amulet with a magic inscription and the "Hand of God," 3rd to 5th centuries (from Syria). *Four times the actual size.*
From the author's collection.

2   Bronze amulet, showing the seven-branched candlestick with palm branch and shofar (obverse), and a Greek inscription, "For the welfare of the Lady Matrona" (reverse). The name Matrona occurs in several Jewish inscriptions. *Actual size.*
From the author's collection.

LAMPS

LAMPS which bear the seven-branched candlestick were found in the Jewish catacombs and elsewhere. The place of origin of these lamps is most probably Palestine, for the earliest examples (3rd century) come from that country. They are closely related to synagogue art.

Lamps were used not only for lighting houses but also as sacrificial offerings in the temples and as funeral gifts. The biblical words, "With lights glorify the Lord" (Isa. 24:15) were explained as referring to the lighting of numerous lamps on holidays. Oil lamps as consecration gifts for synagogues are mentioned in ancient Jewish literature. While in the earliest times lamps consisted simply of open bowls into which the oil was poured (p. 40, no. 3), the wick being set in a pinched-in part, those of later times were closed over and have two small holes, one for filling the lamp with oil and the other for the wick.

The length of lamps such as represented here is from 6.7 to 12 cm.

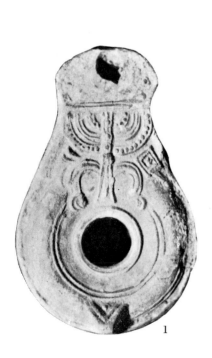

1

2

1,2   Lamps from Syria (1) and Palestine (2), showing the seven-branched candlestick, flanked by the shofar and censer.
No. 1 is from the author's collection; no. 2, from the Monastery of the Flagellation, Jerusalem.
3   Lamp from Ephesus, Asia Minor, showing the seven-branched candlestick with lulav, ethrog, shofar and a matzah such as appeared on the gold glasses (p. 150).
Kunsthistorisches Museum, Vienna.
4   Lamp from Carthage, showing the seven-branched candlestick (about the 5th century). The execution of the candlestick upon lamps found at Carthage is rather primitive. This type spread from there throughout the whole Diaspora; in fact, a lamp of this sort found at Alexandria bears on the back the same potter's mark as a Carthaginian lamp. This type was also found in Rome, and still more curiously, near the old Judengasse at Treves, Germany.
Candlesticks are also found on the lamps of the Jewish Diaspora in Cyprus, Syria. Malta, Sicily and other places.
Vatican Museum, Rome.

1

2

3

4

LAMPS

1   Lamp, showing the seven-branched candlestick with lulav and ethrog; the light-bearing branches and the shaft are depicted in hatched line, the flames rise straight out of the light-bearing arms (from Alexandria, 4th century).

2   Lamp, showing the seven-branched candlestick and amphora (from Syria). American University, Beyrouth, Syria.

3   Lamp of a type found in Cyprus. Museum of Fine Arts, Boston.

4   Bronze lamp, showing the seven-branched candlestick, lulav, ethrog, and shofar, realistically modeled as handle and ornament (from Syria).

GLASS

REMARKABLE GOLD GLASSES have been discovered in the Roman catacombs, most of them in Christian graves. Others have come to light elsewhere in Italy as well as in Atala in Asia Minor, in Germany, and especially in Alexandria, their place of origin. Following earlier Egyptian models, the ones produced in Rome had the design engraved upon gold leaf fixed to the inside of a glass, the surface of the gold leaf being in its turn covered with glass. Many of the Roman gold glasses were found preserved in the lime used to seal the coffins. A few were made as medallions; others were used, as indicated by the inscriptions, for drinking vessels; some may have been votive offerings. In one case a gold glass was used for a tomb inscription.

Gold glasses of this type appear in Rome by the 3rd century; most of the gold glasses probably date from the 4th century. Representations of biblical themes are very popular; scenes from the Old Testament are more numerous than those from the New Testament.

It is open to doubt whether all these gold glasses were produced by Jewish artists, though this is certainly the case in a number of glasses displaying specifically Jewish symbols. The inscriptions, predominantly in Latin, seldom in Greek, usually read "drink and live"; in one instance along with a Greek tomb inscription is found, written in Hebrew, the word "Shalom."

It would seem that the Jews took a prominent part in bringing the art of glass making into Europe. They had learned glass painting from the Phoenicians and Egyptians, and carried on the craft in their homeland as well as in their settlements in Syria and Italy. In the time of the Caesars the Phoenician workshops in Tyre had passed into Jewish hands, and in the 6th century Jewish glassmakers had settled in Constantinople. In the year 687 C.E. Greek workmen emigrated to France where they produced glass in the Jewish manner.

GOLD GLASSES

1   showing a Torah shrine seen from a bird's-eye view, surrounded by a
row of pillars on three sides; steps lead up to the gable-topped shrine. The
two pillars on either side of the shrine are to be regarded either as the
supports on which the curtain was fastened, the latter being omitted
in order not to hinder the view of the shrine, or as modeled after the
two pillars, Jachin and Boaz, of the porch of the Temple at Jerusalem (I
Kings 7:21). In front of the steps stands a seven-branched candlestick,
flanked by vessels for oil or wine, the lulav and ethrog and some other objects
difficult to identify. On the outer side of the pillars are two small buildings
and palm trees. The inscription makes reference to the "house of peace,"
a term used for synagogues also in the Palestinian mosaic inscriptions.
Vatican Museum, Rome.

2   showing a Torah shrine and candlestick with its emblems.
Metropolitan Museum of Art, New York.

GOLD GLASS

showing a seven-branched candlestick with various symbols and a matzah,
the unleavened bread, to the right side of the jar; such a matzah is seen also
on a Jewish lamp from Ephesus (p. 145).
British Museum, London.

GOLD GLASS FROM ROME

showing the Torah shrine upon a pedestal in the form of steps. The shrine is
divided into four compartments, each containing six Torah scrolls; the doors
are open and the curtain is drawn back. In the upper part besides two seven-
branched candlesticks are a shofar, a jar for oil and wine, a lulav and an
ethrog; above the candlesticks, palm branches are seen. The lower section
shows a round table, holding a plate with a fish; a semicircular cushion is
round the table. The scene probably indicates a Sabbath meal. The Latin
inscription is a dedication to "Vitalis" (Hayyim), his wife and son.
Kaiser Friedrich Museum, Berlin.

GOLD GLASS FROM ROME

showing in the upper part a Torah shrine flanked by two lions, emblem of Judah, guarding the divine law, in the lower part two seven-branched candlesticks, lulav, ethrog, oil jars and shofar.
Vatican Museum, Rome.

1   2

GLASSES

1   Pressed glass jar, showing Jewish symbols (probably from Syria).
Museum of Art, Toledo, Ohio.
2   Pressed glass ewer, decorated with Jewish symbols (probably from
Syria).
Museum of Art, Toledo, Ohio.

GLASS MEDALLION

showing the seven-branched candlestick, lulav and ethrog (from Palestine, 4th century); similar medallions were found in Jugoslavia, Cyprus and Tyre. *Three times the actual size.*

From the author's collection.

HEBREW MANUSCRIPTS

IN SUMMER 1947, Hebrew manuscripts written on leather scrolls were found by Bedouins in a cave above the western shore of the Dead Sea. The scrolls, eight of them, and several small fragments, were contained in earthen jugs sealed with bitumen. They present one of the most sensational finds ever made. At the time this book goes to press it appears that the manuscripts date from the 1st and 2nd centuries B.C.E. and contain, among other material, the almost complete Book of Isaiah, hymns similar to the biblical Psalms, parts of a commentary on the Book of Habakkuk, statutes of an unknown Jewish sect, Aramaic fragments of the Book of Enoch, and parts of Genesis, Leviticus, Deuteronomy, Judges and Daniel.

The manuscripts are partly in possession of the Hebrew University, Jerusalem, partly given in custody of the American School of Oriental Research by the Syrian Monastery, Jerusalem.

SCROLL CONTAINING "THE BATTLE BETWEEN THE SONS OF LIGHT AND THE SONS OF DARKNESS"

The hitherto unknown text is an allegorical report from a period preceding the Maccabean period. It describes in detail the various units of the Israelite army, their arms and flags, and even their military police. The scroll, 2.5 m long and .16 m high, was probably deposited before the destruction of the Temple.

FROM THE "THANKSGIVING SCROLL"

A column from a scroll containing thanksgiving hymns resembling in part passages from the Psalms. The script represents early forms of present-day Hebrew.

TWO EARTHEN JARS

which, according to the report of a group of Bedouins who found them in a cave near the Dead Sea, contained some of the scrolls mentioned on p. 155.

LISTS

CHRONOLOGY OF PALESTINIAN ARCHAEOLOGY

1865	Establishment of the Palestine Exploration Fund
1870	Recovery of the Mesha stone
1890	W. M. Flinders Petrie, excavating at Tell-el-Hesi, develops the method of sequence dating; characteristic potsherds, found at different levels, are used to determine chronology
1898	Establishment of the Deutsche Orient Gesellschaft
1902–09	Excavation of Gezer by R. A. S. Macalister
1903–05	Excavation of Megiddo by G. Schumacher
1907–09	Excavations at Jericho by the Deutsche Orient Gesellschaft (Ernst Sellin and Carl Watzinger)
1908 seqq.	Excavation of Samaria by Harvard University (George Andrew Reisner)
1909 seqq.	Excavation of Beth-shemesh by Duncan Mackenzie
1920	Establishment of a Department of Antiquities by the British Mandatory Government of Palestine
1921–33	Excavation of the citadel of Beth-shan under the auspices of the University of Pennsylvania Museum (C. S. Fisher, Alan Rowe, G. M. FitzGerald)
1923–28	Excavations on the Ophel Hill in Jerusalem (R. A. S. Macalister, J. Garrow Duncan, J. W. Crowfoot)
1925–39	Excavation of Megiddo by the Oriental Institute of the University of Chicago (C. S. Fisher, P. L. O. Guy, Gordon Loud)
1925–40	Excavation of the Third Wall of Jerusalem by the Hebrew University, Jerusalem (E. L. Sukenik and L. A. Mayer)
1925 seqq.	Excavations of synagogues (Beth Alpha, el-Hammeh, and others) and Jewish tombs by the Hebrew University, Jerusalem (E. L. Sukenik)
1926–32	Excavation of Tell Beit Mirsim (Kiryath-sepher) by the American School of Oriental Research (M. G. Kyle, W. F. Albright)

1926–35	Excavation of Tel en Nasbeh by the American School of Oriental Research (F. W. Badè)
1928–33	Excavation at Beth-shemesh by the American School of Oriental Research (Elihu Grant)
1929–36	Excavation of Jericho by John Garstang
1931	Excavation at Beth-zur by the American School of Oriental Research (O. R. Sellers, W. F. Albright)
1931–35	Excavation at Samaria by a joint British-American-Hebrew University group (J. W. Crowfoot, E. L. Sukenik, C. S. Fisher)
1932–38	Excavation of Lachish by the Wellcome-Marston expedition (J. L. Starkey); discovery of Hebrew ostraca in 1935 and 1938
1933–43	Archaeological survey of Transjordan by the American School of Oriental Research (Nelson Glueck)
1934	Excavation at Beth-el by the American School of Oriental Research (W. F. Albright, J. L. Kelso)
1936–40	Excavation of Beth-shearim by the Jewish Palestine Exploration Society (B. Maisler)
1937–40	Excavation of Ezion-geber by the American School of Oriental Research (Nelson Glueck)
1944 seqq.	Excavation of Beth-yerah by the Jewish Palestine Exploration Society (M. Stekelis, B. Maisler)
1946	Excavation of Tell Far'a by Roland de Vaux
1947	Discovery of eight scrolls and several fragments containing biblical and other writings written probably not later than the 1st century B.C.E.

BIBLE REFERENCES

Only the most pertinent scriptural passages have been cited.

ARCHAEOLOGICAL SITES

MUSEUMS AND COLLECTIONS

INDEX

ACKNOWLEDGMENTS

MANY ILLUSTRATIONS in this volume are taken from material in the possession of the author. For further illustrations the author is indebted to the following:

Mr. Alinari, Florence; Dr. I. Ben Dor, Jerusalem; Dr. N. Gidal; Dr. Nelson Glueck, Cincinnati; Dr. H. Ingholt; the late Dr. H. Lietzmann; Dr. B. Maisler, Jerusalem; Mr. Raad, Jerusalem; Mr. K. Rosner, Tel Aviv; Mrs. Mirjam Spiro-Schwabe; Dr. E. L. Sukenik, Jerusalem.

American University, Beyrouth; Archives Photographiques d'Art et d'Histoire, Paris; British Museum, London; Keren Hayessod, Jerusalem; Matson Photo Service, Jerusalem; Metropolitan Museum of Art, New York; Musée Gréco-Romain, Alexandria; Museo Nazionale, Rome; Museum of Art, Toledo; Museum of Fine Arts, Boston; Museum of the Hebrew University, Jerusalem; Palestine Exploration Fund, London; Vatican Museum, Rome.

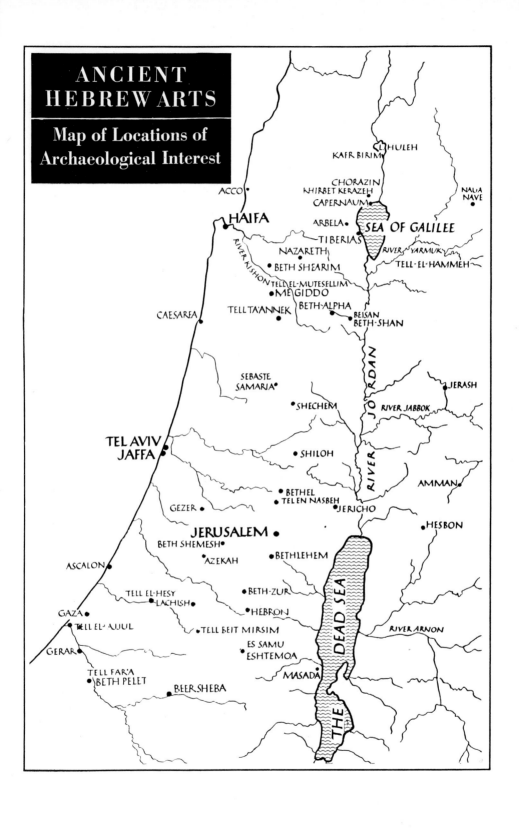

ANCIENT HEBREW ARTS

Map of Locations of Archaeological Interest

EL HULEH
KAFR BIRIM
CHORAZIN
KHIRBET KERAZEH
NALA
NAVE
ACCO
CAPERNAUM
HAIFA
ARBELA
SEA OF GALILEE
TIBERIAS
NAZARETH
RIVER YARMUK
BETH SHEARIM
TELL-EL-HAMMEH
RIVER KISHON
TELL-EL-MUTESELLIM
MEGIDDO
BETH-ALPHA
CAESAREA
TELL TA'ANNEK
BEISAN
BETH-SHAN
SEBASTE
SAMARIA
JERASH
SHECHEM
RIVER JABBOK
JORDAN
TEL AVIV
JAFFA
SHILOH
RIVER
AMMAN
BETHEL
TEL EN NASBEH
GEZER
JERICHO
HESBON
JERUSALEM
BETH SHEMESH
BETHLEHEM
ASCALON
AZEKAH
DEAD SEA
TELL EL-HESY
BETH-ZUR
LACHISH
GAZA
HEBRON
TELL EL-AJJUL
TELL BEIT MIRSIM
RIVER ARNON
GERAR
ES SAMU
ESHTEMOA
TELL FAR'A
BETH PELET
MASADA
THE
BEERSHEBA